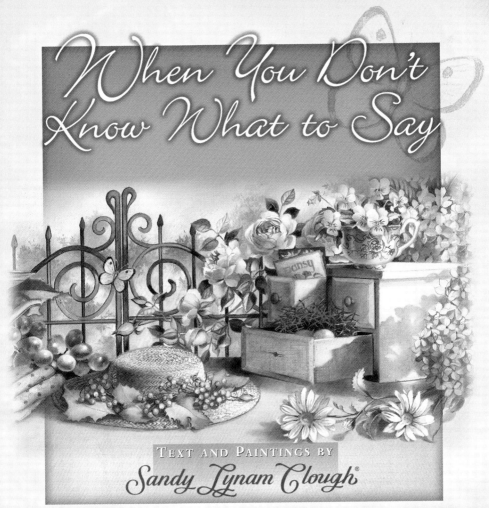

When You Don't Know What to Say

TEXT AND PAINTINGS BY
Sandy Lynam Clough

HARVEST HOUSE PUBLISHERS
Eugene, Oregon

When You Don't Know What to Say

Text Copyright © 2001 by Sandy Lynam Clough
Published by Harvest House Publishers
Eugene, OR 97402

Library of Congress Cataloging-in-Publication Data

Clough, Sandy Lynam, 1948-
When you don't know what to say / Sandy Clough.
p. cm.
ISBN 0-7369-0520-0
1. Consolation. I. Title.

BV4905.2 .C57 2001
248.8'6--dc21

Design and production by Garborg Design Works, Minneapolis, Minnesota

Verses marked AMP are from The Amplified Bible. Old Testament copyright © 1965, 1987 by the Zondervan Corporation. The Amplified New Testament copyright © 1958, 1987 by the Lockman Foundation. Used by permission. Verses marked NAS are from the New American Standard Bible, © 1960, 1962, 1963, 1968, 1971, 1972, 1975, 1977 by The Lockman Foundation. Used by permission. Verses marked TLB are from The Living Bible, copyright © 1971 owned by assignment by Illinois Regional Bank N.A. (as trustee). Used by permission of Tyndale House Publishers, Inc., Wheaton, Illinois 60189. All rights reserved.

Printed in Hong Kong.

03 04 05 06 07 08 09 10 /NG/ 10 9 8 7 6 5 4 3

Dedication

To my dear friend,

Patti Brussat,

a most compassionate

and generous comforter

Sandy Lynam Clough

Contents

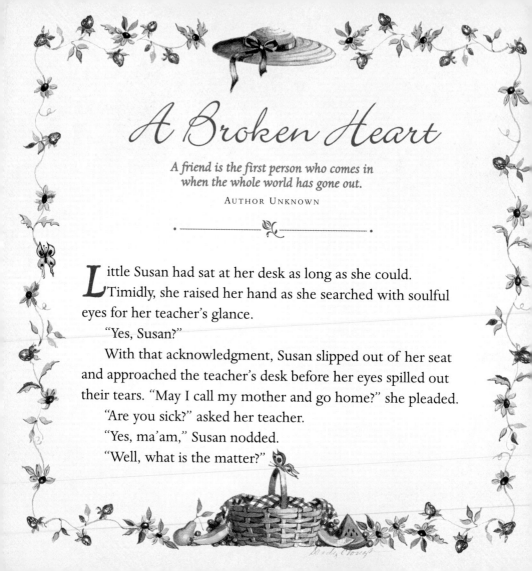

A Broken Heart

*A friend is the first person who comes in
when the whole world has gone out.*

AUTHOR UNKNOWN

———————— ❧ ————————

*L*ittle Susan had sat at her desk as long as she could.
Timidly, she raised her hand as she searched with soulful
eyes for her teacher's glance.

"Yes, Susan?"

With that acknowledgment, Susan slipped out of her seat
and approached the teacher's desk before her eyes spilled out
their tears. "May I call my mother and go home?" she pleaded.

"Are you sick?" asked her teacher.

"Yes, ma'am," Susan nodded.

"Well, what is the matter?"

Susan studied the tops of her shoes for a few seconds and then looked at her teacher and said, "I've got a broken heart."

That tender little story never fails to coax a sympathetic smile from me. All around us, there are people with real broken hearts—hearts so seriously broken that even a mother's comfort would not be enough. The Scriptures say that we are to comfort one another with the same comfort we are comforted with. But how can we help when we feel so helpless? What are the right words to say? What exactly is comfort, anyway?

It is true that to have suffered a specific heartbreak uniquely qualifies me to help someone else with the same or a similar loss. And for years, when I read 2 Corinthians 1:3-4, I had one fervent hope—that I would not have to experience a sampler of suffering (one of each hardship and trial) in order to be able to comfort a variety of people. When my family experienced a job loss and a house fire, I was not excited about building a résumé of suffering!

Now that I (unwillingly) have indeed added to my list of trials and found that the comfort of a loving heavenly Father prevails over all of them and takes their sting away, I see that I was missing the message of the Scripture.

When I read those verses now, the emphasis in my heart is not on my own résumé of suffering, but on the need for comfort that we all have and the equipping that is available to us.

The Amplified Bible says that we experience suffering "...that we may also be able to comfort (console and encourage) those who are in *any* kind of trouble or distress, with the comfort (consolation and encouragement) with which we ourselves are comforted (consoled and encouraged) by God" (emphasis mine).

There is a gift of comfort, and we can all learn how to offer it. The great relief is this: I am not the source of it, nor are you. God is the source of every comfort. The very best consolation and encouragement we can give is to use our own love to point someone to His love.

Having been on the receiving end of both helpful and hurtful "comfort," I have some encouragement to share that I hope will equip you to carry this precious gift of comfort to the breaking hearts around you.

Blessed be the God and Father of our Lord Jesus Christ, the Father of mercies and God of all comfort; who comforts us in all our affliction so that we may be able to comfort those who are in any affliction with the comfort with which we ourselves are comforted by God.

2 CORINTHIANS 1:3-4 NAS

As one whom his mother comforts, so I will comfort you....

ISAIAH 66:13 NAS

9

Too Great for Words

...his suffering was too great for words.

JOB 2:13 TLB

I stood there in the cemetery that summer day after a funeral, part of me not wanting to see my friend. Her child was dead and was never coming back to her. I couldn't tell her I knew how she felt. I was thankful that I didn't know. I couldn't tell her how I would feel if it were my child. I didn't want to know. I needed to say *something* to her that would soothe her pain. But I dreaded my turn to go to her because I had no idea what to say.

Silence is uncomfortable to us, I think, because it makes us feel helpless. Surely, we think, there are words—right words fitly

Sandy Lynam Clough

spoken—for every situation, words that will help. Aren't there?

Sometimes, maybe there aren't.

The book of Job tells us that "when three of Job's friends heard of all the tragedy that had befallen him, they got in touch with each other and traveled from their homes to comfort and console him. …Then they sat upon the ground with him silently for seven days and nights, no one speaking a word; for they saw that his suffering was too great for words" (Job 2:11-13 TLB).

Some suffering is too great for words. How can we know when it is? When someone is in too much emotional pain to receive what I say or when no one is really listening, I need to make friends with silence. In precious, healing quiet, I can share love and concern simply with my presence. There actually is a ministry of "presence." The fact that you are there with the one who is suffering can often help more than any words you say. Holding a hand, bringing a cup of tea, placing a cool cloth on a forehead, or just sitting with someone are all ways of giving the gift of a loving presence. Your friend will always remember that you were there.

"I'm Sorry"

A word fitly spoken and in due season is like
apples of gold in settings of silver.

PROVERBS 25:11 AMP

When a loved one dies, people often offer well-meaning statements to those who are left behind, such as, "She lived a long life." A life is never long enough for those who are grieving their loss. "God must have needed him in heaven" or "God just took her" are not necessarily received with gratitude—and they probably don't turn a lot of people toward God. A grieving person does not want me to justify death. It is enough that I am sorry that it happened.

In fact, when I first mentioned the need for this kind of

book to two of my friends, I said to them, "Actually, this book could have only one page with two words on it: 'I'm sorry.' "

"I'm so sorry." Nothing else, genuinely spoken, is more appropriate for any tragedy or hurtful experience. And sometimes it is all that is appropriate.

Several times I have related to a dear friend of mine hurtful episodes in my life, and each time her response has been, "I'm sorry." She didn't try to guess why something happened, she didn't berate the person who or the circumstance that disappointed me, and she didn't suggest that I could learn a lot from it. I shared the pain in my heart, and with true sympathy she said she was sorry. For me, every time she says it, it is enough.

When saying you're sorry is all that you can say, and you say it with all of your heart, it will be enough for your friend too.

They Know You Don't Know

A man has joy in making an apt answer, and a word spoken at the right moment—how good it is!

PROVERBS 15:23 AMP

---

*B*ecause we serve the One who is the Solution and the Answer, those of us who are Christians tend to feel that we are obligated to bring a solution or an answer to every problem and difficult situation. I know that I have felt helpless and empty-handed without a

practical or spiritual answer for a friend in difficulty. The temptation is to just stay away, feeling useless as well as helpless.

I have good news! Your friend does not want you to wait for a visit until you can comfort her with an answer. I'll let you in on a secret. Your friend knows you don't know the answer. She does not expect you to have the power to change her situation.

When I struggled with three different eye surgeries and the fear of losing my sight, I never expected any of my friends to have the answers to my vision problems. I knew they could not restore my damaged vision. Only the Lord could do that. What I wanted from them was love, concern, fellowship, encouragement, and prayer.

The next time someone you love is in a difficult circumstance that just doesn't make any sense, feel free to just run to her with your love—and without an answer to the dilemma. It's okay to say that you don't understand it and you don't know. She already knows that. She just needs you.

Good Questions

*To him who is about to faint and despair,
kindness is due from his friend...*

JOB 6:14 AMP

*A*s much as we would like to have answers to give our hurting
friends, good questions give us the opportunity to offer
comfort by listening.

In my experience, I found that questions from friends who
were showing their concern allowed me to voice my traumas and
questions. And that allowed me to talk about my new, uncomfortable circumstances. If you ask the questions, please prepare to be
sincerely patient for the answers and to have a deep tolerance for
tears or even complaining. As my own heart healed over a
number of months, I finally lost interest in talking about my

losses. But this happened only after my friends and family had practiced the ministry of "listening" for my sake. It is an act of mercy to let a hurting soul tell you what has happened to her world.

Some caring questions are:

- Do you want to tell me what happened?
- Are you afraid?
- What are your days like?
- What concerns you the most about this situation?
- Are you able to sleep?
- Are you afraid to be alone?
- How do you want me to pray for you?
- Can I give you a hug?

There are also practical questions that help a hurting person continue to function. Don't ask her to let you know if she needs anything. She won't. Be specific and practical.

Some helpful practical questions are:

- May I watch your children or pick them up for you?
- Do you need me to make any calls or notify anyone for you?
- Would you like for me to be here to answer the phone?
- May I bring clean clothes to the hospital for you?
- May I drive you to the doctor or pick up your medicine?
- Would you join us for the holidays?
- What time would you like dinner?

When you don't know the answers,
let your questions bring comfort.

*My friend is one who considers
my need before my deserving.*

AUTHOR UNKNOWN

Sandy Lynam Clough

Personal Surrender

As clay is in the potter's hand, so are you in my hand.

JEREMIAH 18:6 TLB

"Tell the Lord you're willing to be blind, and the devil can't make you afraid of it anymore." This was the advice a friend gave me, hoping to free me from my fear of blindness. I was having enough trouble accepting the amount of damage I had in one eye as irreversible. I could not bring myself to say, "I'm willing to be blind." I don't think my lips could have even formed the words.

Please don't suggest any surrender to a hurting person that you have not been willing to make yourself. Ask yourself if you're willing to be blind or to die or to be divorced before you suggest that someone else should be. It is true that these deep surrenders bring us close to the heart of God. But such surrenders are easier said than sincerely done. He has to gently draw us there as we trust Him more and more. Although surrender is necessary, pointing out the need for it can be a hard saying. When hard sayings need to be said, they can best be said by those who have experienced their own suffering and surrender.

Scripture should be used carefully. Although it is described as a sword, it should not be a club! "Though He slay me, yet will I trust Him" is to me a wonderfully awesome verse, but it should never be used to measure the faith of a suffering saint. That depth of surrender is the

Holy Spirit's job. People in distress have enough to handle without a friend suggesting that God might also want to kill them—and the least they can do is to be willing!

I had to face a personal version of the attitude of that verse. If the Lord were willing for me to lose my sight, would I trust Him with my eyes? I remember very clearly the day I released my eyes to the Lord. It took six months for me to get to that point, but it was a bedrock event for me.

Surrender to the will of God is a very real issue for someone in crisis. For me, it was seeing the absolute goodness and trustworthiness of our Lord that made my surrender to His will possible. Only His love can make it easy.

Sandy Lynam Clough

Sandy Lynam Clough

Sandy Lynam Clough

"You're My Hero"

*The Lord God has given Me the tongue of a disciple
and of one who is taught, that I should know how to speak
a word in season to him who is weary.*

ISAIAH 50:4 AMP

I remember this line from a children's book my boys had
when they were young: "Job, Job, what did you do to make
the Lord so mad at you?"

Most of us are sensitive enough not to blame our friends
for their trials or suggest that what they're experiencing is
God's punishment. However, to say that someone was chosen
for a trial or difficulty can sound almost as hurtful. How does
it feel to hear, "You were specially chosen to be handicapped"

or "God knew He could trust you with it"? Nobody asks to be that special! Oh, to be ordinary!

Eighteen months into my personal struggle I was finally able to write this in my journal: "Lord, I have been chosen for this trial. Help me cooperate with You for the final results that You want from this." I knew it was true, but it didn't make me happy. It was not a gleeful statement. It was simply a recognition and resignation. Today I am able to thank God for all the difficulties, even those that remain.

I am grateful for what He allowed to happen and what He chose for me.

It is not for us to look at our friends and say what is chosen and what is permitted. What is needed is the encouragement of "strength for today and bright hope for tomorrow" found in the hymn "Great Is Thy Faithfulness."

It is a tremendous encouragement for someone to say to a hurting friend, "You're doing a great job." For one of the greatest fears in a trial is failing—especially failing as a Christian. I remember thinking how people would be so disappointed in me if they knew how difficult a time I was having trusting God. Somehow, I thought a better Christian would be able to just say, "Praise God," and smile and go on. How much it encouraged me when my friend Patti would tell me that I was her hero and that I was doing so well! I still didn't think I was doing all that well, but hearing that *she* thought so encouraged me and made me feel so much better!

Does your friend need a cheerleader? If she's hurting, she does! You can be that for her. There are many encouraging things you could say to her: "You're facing a hard thing—you're doing well." "I trust you—I know you'll make the right decision." "I admire your courage." "You're a good example to me." And especially, "You're my hero!"

What We Know to Be True

Do not fear, for I am with you: Do not look anxiously about you,
for I am your God. I will strengthen you, I will help you. Surely,
I will uphold you with my righteous right hand.

ISAIAH 41:10 NAS

My fifteen-year-old son finished his conversation with his friend and put the phone down. "Well, what did Brad have to say?" I casually quizzed as I passed through the room.

"He said that Jennifer killed herself this morning."

I was stunned. Surely this was some kind of sick telephone game some teenager was playing. I quickly called the secretary

Sandy Lynam Clough

at the school, who told me that what my son had heard was indeed true.

As part of their regular nightly prayer time, my husband had always told our boys that they would never have a problem that he and I and the Lord couldn't handle. This situation was definitely one we had not anticipated. As we pulled together as a family to walk through this tragedy, feeling deep grief over the loss of our child's friend, there was one question in my mind: Would my son blame God for Jennifer's death and have a bitterness in his heart?

My question was soon answered. The next day at school, Brad told my son, "God took her."

"God did not kill her," my son replied, "she killed herself."

When I heard that, I knew that he would be all right. And if his friend Brad—a Christian—had thought through his own statement, he would have realized that God does not shoot children! But I'm sure that he, as we all have, had heard God blamed for many tragedies.

At any time when God's comfort is the only thing that can really help, it is cruel to pin all the blame on Him as the cause of the pain.

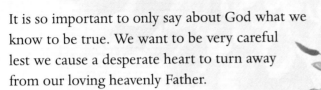

It is so important to only say about God what we know to be true. We want to be very careful lest we cause a desperate heart to turn away from our loving heavenly Father.

Heartbreaking circumstances are the emotional earthquakes of our lives. But God's Word tells us that He is our rock and there is no unrighteousness in Him (Psalm 92:15). By marking verses in a Bible that declare the Lord is good and trustworthy, or by compiling a list of those Scriptures for a hurting friend, we may lead someone whose world has been shaken to a safe and solid place of rest in His Word. It is there that we are reassured by God Himself of His faithful heart and His precious love for us, when nothing else makes sense.

A Kind Touch

If a friend of mine... gave a feast, and did not invite me to it, I should not mind a bit....But if...a friend of mine had a sorrow and refused to allow me to share it, I should feel it most bitterly.

OSCAR WILDE

As my hairdresser washed my hair, I asked her what were some good things people had said to her during the difficult times in her life. As she began, "The worst thing..." I realized I was starting to see a pattern. I had been informally surveying my friends on this topic for weeks, and almost nobody had been able to tell me anything good that anyone had said, any words that had made a difference to them.

What were some of the worst things people had said to them? "I know how you feel." "You'll get over it." Several women in the salon that night agreed that what had meant the most to them in difficult times was silence and a kind touch.

My dear friend Gerrie lost her young grandson after a long illness. When I asked her what people had said to her that comforted her the most, this is what she wrote: " 'Touching' has made the top of my list for what was significant on hard days. A nurse who held me close and let me cry in the hospital. A young man who put his strong arm around my shoulders at a church altar while I prayed and cried. The young lady who held my hands when I wept loudly in a group. My daughter patting me to comfort me. It's very curious to me—I don't remember any words."

A kind touch says a lot—an arm around the shoulders, holding a hand, patting an arm. No words are necessary.

Prayer

The worst sorrows in life are not in its losses
and misfortunes, but in its fears.

A.C. BENSON

———— ❧ ————

Elizabeth was in her garden early, carefully clipping fresh flowers. As she selected each blossom and shook the dew off it, she prayed for her friend Colleen. After she had enough for a beautiful bouquet, she gathered the flowers into a vase. When she got to work that morning, she secretly placed the bouquet on Colleen's desk, for Colleen was going through a very difficult time. Elizabeth wanted her to know that someone was thinking of her.

Colleen didn't know who brought the flowers, and before they could wilt, each bouquet was anonymously replaced by a fresh one, over and over. This went on for a long time before Colleen discovered that Elizabeth was her encourager.

Elizabeth admitted to Colleen, "I don't know that I have any words that could help you. But I can do this for you, and while I pick the flowers, I pray for you."

How wise Elizabeth is! She knows that no matter how fresh and beautiful the flowers are, in a few days they will fade. But her prayers for Colleen will never fade.

"I prayed for you today." What an

encouragement! For me, it is an evidence of God's love that someone is praying for me.

Several months ago, I faced not a tragic time but a challenging and very stressful time. In the midst of one long weekend, I was trying to finish all the paintings for a new book, was scheduled to do five signings at a gift show, and had several meetings and a business dinner for twenty-five people in my home on my agenda. How would I be able to handle it all? Not everyone around me was convinced I could—and I was secretly inclined to agree with them! But I did make it through everything, despite getting little sleep and being exposed to the flu several times. In the next four days I even finished my book on time! What a relief!

A short time later, I received a note from a

friend in Florida whom I had not seen or talked to in many years. This is what Sherrie wrote:

Just a note to let you know the Lord woke me up to pray for you last week and reminded me to intercede daily for you. It was my pleasure. I just wanted you to know that He was thinking of you and loves you so much. Many times we do not know why He is calling others to pray and sometimes it's because we have just cried out "HELP, Lord!"

According to my calculations, she prayed when I really needed help! If the Lord prompts you to pray for a person and you let her know that you did, you demonstrate not only your own love but also God's very personal care for her. If you don't know what to do or say for someone, pray. The Lord knows exactly what she needs.

Walking with a Limp

Have you been asking God what He is going to do? He will never tell you. God does not tell you what He is going to do. He reveals to you who He is.

OSWALD CHAMBERS

When someone I know is in desperate need of a physical healing or a restoration, I want to pray for a miracle that will bring a happy ending. But I must be careful not to promise a perfect outcome if the Lord has not assured me of that.

Sometimes God heals, sometimes He doesn't. That doesn't mean that His power to heal comes and goes, nor does it mean that His love ebbs and flows for you and for me. What God can do in a person's spirit in a tender time may be much more significant than what changing their circumstances would do.

In the Bible, Jacob's limp was a sign that he had wrestled with God. He was a changed man, but not a perfect specimen. In fact, he was so different that his name was not even to remain the same.

One evening as we sat around the dining room table, my son Samuel said, "I'm not sure but that some are always supposed to have a limp." He was talking about me, and I knew exactly what he meant. Yes, I have a "limp" in my eye that has not been healed. It will always remind me of how God miraculously rescued me from a nightmare of fear of blindness and gave me peace, new joy, new purpose, and a confidence in Him—without healing me. Yes, it's possible to have an encounter with God, be blessed, and still walk away with a limp.

There are occasionally days when I say, "Lord, this is hard," and I think wistfully of the healing and normal vision I would like to have now. But there is never a day when I would trade what He has done for me personally in that affliction for the option of physical healing.

What wonderful encouragement there is in the saying, "He gives the very best to those who leave the choice to Him."

Time

W hen my friend Mary returned to work after the loss of her mother, she walked into her office to find a big, soft, fluffy teddy bear sitting in her chair. She didn't even have to touch the bear to feel the hug from her friends.

It's not uncommon for someone who has experienced a loss or tragedy to have to return to a routine of school or work while they're still feeling anything but normal.

Still emotionally fragile, simply talking may be difficult for a hurting person. The fear of losing emotional control and breaking down can be very real. This is a perfect time for those of us who like to talk for a friend! Imagine that I was the first person to see

Mary in her office that morning and that shortly after Julie dropped by to express her sympathy, saying, "I'm so sorry for your loss, Mary. We missed you and we're happy to have you back."

As the tears well up in Mary's eyes, I have a chance to rescue her: "I was just telling Mary how much we all have felt her loss and kept her in our hearts while she was gone. Why don't we all eat lunch together today to welcome her back?" All Mary has to do is nod. Lunch with her friends will be a welcome diversion.

Whether it is a death, a sick child, a job loss, a health crisis, or a marriage crisis, giving a friend a short diversion can bring a welcome breath of normalcy and a temporary respite that lifts the spirit. A card, a telephone call, a movie, a lunch out, or a small gift are time and money well spent. Your continuous attention and love may keep your friend from feeling abandoned, especially if difficulties have removed her from her normal schedule and contact with people.

If you don't have time to do a lot—and most of us don't—try to be regular in what you do, whether it's once a week or once a month. My friend Patti made it a point to take me to lunch once a month and have "girlfriend" time to talk about my situation. I was always encouraged after our time together.

It's important not to give up. Understand that some trials last a long time, but that time alone will not necessarily ease the pain.

If some time has already passed before you even knew of someone's hurt, or if you've been slow to respond because you didn't know what to do, it's never too late to care and show your love.

Believe me, every man has his secret sorrows,
which this world knows not, and oftentimes
we call a man cold when he is only sad.

LONGFELLOW

"God Loves You"

The eternal God is a dwelling place,
and underneath are the everlasting arms.

DEUTERONOMY 33:27 NAS

There is no doubt in my mind that God created me, called me, and equipped me to be a Christian artist. So why did He allow the retina to detach in one of my eyes, and why hasn't He healed it? Aren't those the two questions in our hearts when we suffer or see someone else suffering? "Lord, why did You let this happen?" and "Why don't You do something about it?"

I spent weeks in the book of Psalms writing down the verses that said God is good and that He hears me, watches me, and has a plan for me. As I did that, a confidence in Him and His character developed that caused those questions to fade away and to take my fears with them. His comfort replaced my nightmare. What was left? Peace, joy, and a desire to get on with the wonderful plans He has for my life.

But when one of my friends became seriously ill, the questions I had already settled for myself returned. Why did she get sick? Why

hadn't she been healed? I woke up one morning and although I knew I had slept, I felt I had wrestled with these questions all night long. As I prayed, I confessed to the Lord, "I don't know how to think about this situation. Please give me Your thoughts." Three words could answer my question and help me deal with the situation. The three words I wanted to hear were: "She will live."

But the three words I heard softly in my heart were the words I needed: "I love her."

If you had asked me fifteen minutes before if God loved her, I could have given you an academic answer. Of course He does—He loves everybody. Now, His love for her was so personal to me. I knew He was with her, no matter what she was going through, and for the first time I was really able to put her in His hands.

Yes, He loves her. He loves me. And He loves you. What are the right words when you don't know what to say? "God loves you." When we use our own love to say it in every practical and sensitive way we can, it is our privilege to present the gift of comfort to the broken hearts around us.

The Spirit of the Lord [is] upon Me, because He has anointed me, [the Anointed One, the Messiah] to preach the good news (the Gospel) to the poor; He has sent Me to announce release to the captives and recovery of sight to the blind, to send forth as delivered those who are oppressed [who are downtrodden, bruised, crushed and broken down by calamity].

LUKE 4:18 AMP

Words of Comfort Supported by Scripture

"We cannot see Him in these circumstances; we must look for him in His Word."
JOB 42:5

"I will carry this burden with you."
GALATIANS 6:2

"I won't forget you."
ISAIAH 49:15,16

"I am committing myself to pray for you."
PSALM 4:3

"The Lord hears and sees your weeping. He hears your prayers."
PSALM 6:8

"You can call me anytime."
PSALM 116:12

"I care about you. You are special to me."
JOHN 13:34,35

"I love you."
1 JOHN 4:7,8

"The Lord has not left you."
PSALM 9:10

"The Lord is not finished with you."
PSALM 138:8